THE LION'S SHARE

Animal Idioms
(A Multicultural Book)

By Troon Harrison
Illustrated by Dmitry Fedorov

Language Lizard
Basking Ridge

For English audio and resources for teaching idioms,
see the last page of this book.

The Lion's Share
Copyright © 2020 Language Lizard
Published by Language Lizard
Basking Ridge, NJ 07920
info@LanguageLizard.com

Visit us at www.LanguageLizard.com

First edition 2020

Library of Congress Control Number: 2020904810

ISBN: 978-1-951787-02-8 (Print)
ISBN: 978-1-951787-03-5 (Ebook)

WHAT IS AN IDIOM?

An idiom is a phrase that says one thing but means something different. An idiom can be a quick way of saying something complicated. Knowing idioms will help you to understand and speak English fluently. This book contains idioms about animals.

ANTS IN YOUR PANTS

Meaning: Not being able to stay still

I can tell you are excited to see your grandmother because you have **ants in your pants.**

GETS MY GOAT

Meaning: Feeling annoyed

It really **gets my goat** when my sister eats all the snacks.

BUSY AS A BEE

Meaning: To work hard and quickly at a job

When Mom cleans the house, she is busy as a bee.

RAINING CATS AND DOGS

Meaning: Heavy rain that makes you very wet

I forgot to bring my umbrella and now it is raining cats and dogs.

HOLD YOUR HORSES

Meaning: Be patient and don't be hasty

Hold your horses! You can join your friends after you finish your chores.

GET MY DUCKS IN A ROW

Meaning: To be well prepared for something that is going to happen

Before moving to another country, I had to get my ducks in a row.

BUTTERFLIES IN MY STOMACH

Meaning: Feeling nervous or excited

When I sing on stage, I get **butterflies** in my stomach.

16

TAKE THE BULL BY THE HORNS

Meaning: Being brave, facing up to a challenge

I was scared to compete, but my coach told me to **take the bull by the horns.**

AS THE CROW FLIES

Meaning: The straight, direct route

The man thought it was not far to the valley as the crow flies.

UNTIL THE COWS COME HOME

Meaning: Doing something for a very long time

There is so much to sweep, I'll be working until the cows come home.

21

AT A SNAIL'S PACE

Meaning: Doing something very slowly

When I'm late for school, Mom says I am moving **at a snail's pace.**

SMELL A RAT

Meaning: Feeling that something is wrong

A man said the bridge was safe, but I smelled a rat.

LET THE CAT OUT OF THE BAG

Meaning: Giving away a secret

I wanted the party to be a surprise, but I accidentally **let the cat out of the bag**.

THE LION'S SHARE

Meaning: Having the most of something

I tried to cut the pizza in half, but Dad told me to take **the lion's share.**

Visit <u>www.LanguageLizard.com/Animal-Idioms</u> for additional resources for teaching and learning English idioms, including:

- English audio of this book
- Multicultural lesson plans for use in the classroom or at home
- Information on the origin of the idioms in this book
- Additional animal idioms with their meaning, usage, and origin
- Information on idiom translations and idioms in other languages

This book is part of the **Language Lizard Idiom Series**.

Visit **www.LanguageLizard.com** for a complete listing of the titles in this series and available languages.